I'm Dancing
As Fast As I Can

Charol Messenger

Note for Librarians: A cataloguing record for this book is available from Library and Archives Canada at www.collectionscanada.ca/amicus/index-e.html

ISBN 1-4120-7253-0

Printed in Victoria, BC, Canada. Printed on paper with minimum 30% recycled fibre. Trafford's print shop runs on "green energy" from solar, wind and other environmentally-friendly power sources.

Offices in Canada, USA, Ireland and UK

This book was published *on-demand* in cooperation with Trafford Publishing. On-demand publishing is a unique process and service of making a book available for retail sale to the public taking advantage of on-demand manufacturing and Internet marketing. On-demand publishing includes promotions, retail sales, manufacturing, order fulfilment, accounting and collecting royalties on behalf of the author.

Book sales for North America and international:

Trafford Publishing, 6E–2333 Government St.,

Victoria, BC v8t 4p4 CANADA

phone 250 383 6864 (toll-free 1 888 232 4444)

fax 250 383 6804; email to orders@trafford.com

Book sales in Europe:

Trafford Publishing (uk) Limited, 9 Park End Street, 2nd Floor

Oxford, UK ox1 1hh UNITED KINGDOM

phone 44 (0)1865 722 113 (local rate 0845 230 9601)

facsimile 44 (0)1865 722 868; info.uk@trafford.com

Order online at:

trafford.com/05-2148

10 9 8 7 6 5 4 3 2 1

Reviews

"Pure aesthetic delight. Some seem to be genius. I tried to imagine myself writing any of these . . . and I could not do it. ALL are truly inspired. A museum of fine art where the whole collection tells a very personal story. Looking at each poem is like standing in front of a great work of art, staring, thinking, trying to fathom it . . . then finally seeing it, and walking away much more enlightened and pleased."
– Barbara Munson, ghostwriter and editor

"Sometimes raw, and always honest, Charol Messenger's poems illuminate the human condition. They remind me of what it's like to fall in love, and have your heart broken—again and again. I especially enjoyed following the growth of a young woman enveloped in the world of her senses through to her spiritual awakening. Charol's honesty and willingness to make herself vulnerable through her writing are unusual and moving." – Susan Paturzo, software designer

Books by Charol Messenger

The New Humanity: Our Destiny
Prophecies of Global Social Transformation
A personal guide
NEW HUMANITY series, Vol. I

I'm Dancing As Fast As I Can
Memoir

Coming Soon

Recognizing Your Natural Intuition
A 30-year collection of techniques, tools, and strategies
for connecting to your inner knowing self

Petals of Self-Discovery
The Soul Path to Your Inner Knowing Self
The steps, stages, and phases of the spiritual life
SOUL PATH series, Vol. I

The Hidden
A light suspense paranormal novel
set in New Orleans and the Louisiana bayou Aug.-Sept. 2004

Wings of Light
The Four Angels Who Help You Every Day
and Finding a Lost Loved One
ANGELS SPEAK series, Vol. I

Dedicated to

my sister, Jo, my best friend,

and Keith, a lifelong true friend

Cover Design: Victor J. Crapnell, artdepartmentdesign.com
Cover Photo: Ric Frazier, "Underwater Leap"
Author Photo: Nickey Russel, photographer; Gena Subia, stylist: glamourshotsusa.com
Book Editor: thewritingdoctor.biz
Editorial Advisor: Barbara Munson, munsoncommunications.com

Contents

NOW

NOW

Confounding life,
plummeting faults,
egregious weights of my human condition.
Confusion, doubt, overconcern, oversensitivity
    at my inability to maintain the higher road.

Moment by moment
sucked up
wrung out
strangled peace
into the vortex
of the world's pendulum:
be this, be that;
am this, am that.
    Am what?

Bewildered,
suspicions lay into me
    my entire life.
Inescapable.
Unshaken.
    No matter the wisdom attained
    and sought.
    No matter the desire to be good
        fair
        genuine.
    No matter the truth:
        inner relationship with divinity,
        moments of deepest peace,
            the sustenance of my life.

More than once
sweetness has filled me.
I have seen my Potential and my Purpose.
  Touched it.
  More than once.

Inner knowing
  at times.
Assurance
  at times.
The inner guide,
my comforter through it all,
soothing the deep wounds of my soul and human heart.

Living in-between:
  Personality engulfed with unreason,
  and the Self blissed with cherished insight

into the wholeness of the human experience:
    Our purpose divinity.
    The truth of what we are.
    The calm that *is* attainable.

BEFORE

COLLIE OF MY YOUTH

Echoing his name across windswept countryside,
I shortly see him lolloping up the dusty road,
across the buffalo-grass wild pasture to the weathered wired gate,
his puppy paws eagerly patting the dried cracked earth,
his yellow hair shimmering under the fiery West Texas sunset.
I kneel and he rushes up to me,
nudging enthusiastically with a cold wet nose,
licking me all over with wet kisses.

Dismal evening
silent emptiness
darkened gate
lonely road
desolate form

earthed beneath a rugged cross
forged by my tears,
enrapturing his too-brief life into my being.

Years have passed
yet I still yearn for my simple trusting friend
to be a child with.

Searched and found
a new companion,
a rollicking new friend
who tosses his head to and fro,
chases his tail
and comes when I say go.

MY DOGGONE DOG

Scraggly ten-pound brute of bark,
he pounces, nuzzles, growls, then larks,
while in his eyes there gleams an impish spark.

My every step is in his way.
He snaps, in fun, my feet to sway.
My ten toes giggle, wiggle, all in play.

Then with a whim of cat-like spree,
he races through the house with glee
and suddenly he plops himself on me.

He drops across my open book
and yelps in earnest for a look
of rapt attention and a gentle stroke.

A runt-sized rascal worn from yap,
he limply lays upon my lap
and settles still to briefly take a nap.

A few hushed moments lapse, he steals
a smile, while sleeping he appeals
for quiet chuckles and applause. I kneel.

A mischievous spritely elf, he's frequently a pest,
and every single day each moment is a test.
Though perfect he isn't, by far, he's still the doggone best.

EPITAPH OF A MARRIAGE

My Husband
Was Not the Lover
I Left Behind

SECOND LOVE

Beautiful man
grey temples
liquid dreamy eyes.
Black turtleneck sweater
tweed jacket
melodious poet voice.
Spellbinding me.

HONORABLE YOU

Hypnotized at first glance of you,
handsome Barney Miller look-alike
teaching the night creative-writing class.

Snowflake days, Christmas carols, singing,
holding candles up into the night,
coffee breaks, wines, cheeses, parking lots.
Honorable you.

Pining for you,
passionate part-time writer-teacher-minister married.

Sleeping not with my husband.
On the couch alone,

Johnny Mathis into the night.
Fantasizing.

Book of rhymes,
miniature bottle of Mateus wine I gave you,
telling you I loved you,
writing long poems to you
    for the class.
Honorable you.

Your wisdom, will power
fleeting moments
fleeting touches
    opening my heart.
Honorable you.

AURA OF LOVE

A new light is in me
flickering
glowing.
An aura of blushing love,
awakening
new desire.

Thinking of you, I smile,
and warm all over.
Real love or not,
a doorway
into myself.

MIRROR IN MY MIND

The depth of your eyes filling my mind.
I cannot escape you

and we can never be near.

you

I tucked you away,
a friend.
Still, your liquid grey eyes embrace me,
your melodic voice caresses me,
the memory of your touch warms me.
I don't feel like just a friend

and I can't unlove you.

DEPRESSION

Oh, that I were a silver ship
gliding silently across a twilight sea of space,
spilling wisps of angels hair upon the tranquil face
of the dusking summer sunset's fading lace.

Oh, that I were a silver ship
threading one last strand of silver-clouded staircase
up the dimming softness of the cobalt blue-gray day,
I would serenely smile at life and sail away
    far far away
and disappear into the starring bay.

Oh, that I were a silver ship
raising my unseen wings in life
    as well as in wishful dreams,
freedom from these grinding pressures,
    this parasitic leech
    sapping my strength and peace of mind.

                  Oh, that I were . . .

GOOD MAN

Parched and desolate
loving you.
　　Brief touches.
　　You knowing when to part.

Sensual man
righteous,
loving me innocently,
with restraint.
More than I.

I no longer belong to my husband.

Romance Marriage

MY ONCE TRUE LOVE

Handsome young Amarillo airman,
look-alike Superman Christopher Reeve,
six-four, large hands, flat top, brilliant blue eyes,
All American clean-cut regular Joe.

In love with the image, not the man:
sports, beer, dirty jokes. Alcoholic.
Cinderella dreams.

Your '57 white Chevy Impala,
us driving from barren dusty windy Amarillo
to your luscious blue-green God's country east
to the roach-infested apartment with the sloping unpolished wooden floor.
Newlyweds.

Escaped drugs, free sex, acid rock, riots, revolutions, the hippie life.
Escaped authoritative adult parental power:
    to marriage games
        outside ourselves
    to plans:
        house, yard, trees, dogs, your friends, your family
           they became my own
        three-and-one-half acres for the house we never built.

Void conversation.
Uncommon values.
Growing up pain.

Unspoken vacuous disintegration.
Nervous anxiety, migraines, valiums.
Spiraling downward.

Seeking validity of myself.
A rim of light
    insatiably pursued.

Agatha Christie mysteries, Ruth Montgomery, Edgar Cayce. Metaphysics.
"That stuff will make you crazy."
    You shut me out.
It's the only thing keeping me sane,
    I unspeak.

Drifting.
Separation dream
    dream dream, dream dream, dream dream, dream dream . . .
    three years.

Sideswiped, unconscious.
Migraines 24/7, taut drawn, cold clammy, pressure pulsing,
reverberating zipping erupting exploding
     unceasing!

Willowy pale girl
smudges of mascara
thoughts spinning tumbling.
     Avalanche unloosed!
     Clouding.

Silent Man
drawn away from me
     dreams
     no faces
     lost

I can't find my way home.

Abandoned.
Writing my companion, my world.

Group therapy unleashes me.

You never said I love you.

ESCAPE

Dark.
Familiar footsteps.
Curtains draw back beside my bed.
The shadow stares,
leers an insane curse,
raises a mountain fist,
crashes down,
shattering lusty limbs and breasts,
bloodash and bone.

Imagination is a scary thing.

HUSBAND END

The fearful necessity
    to be honest.

Tall handsome good man
stubborn silent,
you knew.

I didn't want to see you
    talk
    be near you.
Not now.

I know now it wasn't love.
It was a childhood dream,
suffocated in apathy
and illusion.

DIVORCE

No turning back.
Pressure cooking me.

AFTERSHOCK

The dreadful truth.
Dreams, wishes, hopes.
 Make believe.

Tossing turning, up down, up down, up down.
Could it be? Could it be? Could it?
 If only.

What if I change my life . . . and disappear?

UMBILICAL CORD

Family I never knew,
you call now?
Home for a visit?

It isn't home.
Home is nowhere.
No one.

DOUBT

Is it just compassion I feel when I look at you?
You are sad in a way I've not seen before.
You ask nothing of me,
as if you're beaten.
Do you know you've lost me?

I'd made up my mind
after months of indecision.
Not love, you filled a need.
I don't hate you.

Sifting through feelings,
not wearing the rings.
The hand feels naked.

I was positive I was ready.
Do I just feel sorry for you?
Or am I looking for escape?
From what?
    I don't want to be alone.

One Fantasy to Another

PARTING

Goodbye
is a lonely wind in the night,
sweeping silently
through black empty streets of early morning.
Silence itself holds unshed tears.

Lights blink out.
Fingers intertwine and squeeze.
No words,
only a look, a touch
saying:
I hope we meet again.

LIMBO

Flying,
swallowed in blue and white,
unnoticed from the patches far below.
Saying goodbye
again.

Between two lives:
    a holiday, a new man, a new bond,
    and home, a different kind of life.

LIGHT

Sunset seas of lilac, aqua, peach
flow from the burning yellow ball.

Purple shadows, midnight blues
drop dusk
into opal blackness.

The earth extends endlessly,
half the circle glowing . . .
a city's incandescent life
reaching across eternal night.

I am the moon rising through darkness.

REMEMBER ME

No steeple bells ring out with wedding cheer,
no turtle doves are winging near
to tell me of your love.
You are not here.

Cherish my lock of amber hair.
Remember me, my Pisces dear.

A CURTAIN RISES

I still see
your soft grey eyes
touching me,
hear our whispers
floating through the night,
feel my breath
pillowed against your cheek.
Relearning love.

WINTER SOUL

The kiss of winter's breath chills my longing soul.
I am a January tree
reaching naked fingers
into the smoky grey
unbroken horizon of sky earth lake,
cloaked by mist
memories
grey eyes grey hair grey smiles
grey hearts.

Shifting
a foot,
        cloaked
        fogged,
steadying myself.

Winter
        absorbing
        muting
        bare
        barren.

I am winter.

LIBERATED WOMAN

SINGLE AGAIN

dead for a time

Endlessly on the fling
the spice of life
seeking the special love.
Numerous men.
    Woman child.

ENJOYING sex again.
Self-pampering.
Living ALONE.

Self-indulging
wine mellow giggles
uneaten dinners.

Sexy sensual
delicate sensitive
dingy silly smart
fearless afraid.

Looking for a job
reading in bed
no roommate, leaving dishes, sleeping 'til noon.
Teaching my pet rock to play dead. Being heard.

Smoky dens, disco, rock n' roll,
sweltering bodies writhing swinging hips,
ski bunnies, crowds, laughing, short tall fat thin,
Margueritas, Tom Collins, Screwdrivers, hot *glug*,
beef tips, sausages, baked beans, chicken gizzards.
Hearts.
Go with the vibes, the feeling, the moment.
Creature comfort.

Men helping.
Opening wine bottles, installing locks,
holding my hand, face, breasts.
Men's hands.

Facing family.
Moving.
Restless.

Series of pets.
Series of men.
    A hundred years.

The pill.
Therapy.

SIX NIGHTS OF INSOMNIA

Long bleak hours
in empty bed.
Guilts, lonelys, poor little me's.
Music of the night, Rod McKuen,
round and round inside my head.
Starting a page in Zolar's book on dreams.
Rearranging some books I have not read.
Sorrowing that you are far away,
anguishing over my doldrum job,
thinking I should write.

Three a.m. I take a pill. Give up the fight.

MASQUERADE

My name is Medusa,
throbbing to the
clatterbang-sooth-my-savage-soul
writhing immutable sounds of sin.

My body laps up leers
and slurs of kisses,
but my Helenflesh masks cinders.

Disrobe my flesh
and weep to find the gypsy
I was born.

She is no more.

ENCHANTMENT

High-cheeked, black-haired, firm young man,
your home is an enchanting forest.

Inner sanctuary:
warm mist, a thousand plants and owls
    on walls, doors, floors, plaques, statues, drawings, sequined, crocheted,
    macramed, feathered, glassed, in pots among leaves and leaves and leaves.
Homey kitchen, emptied plates of ham, baked bread, banana pie.

Outer sanctuary:
    a garden here, another there,
    St. Francis of Assisi, Mary blessing the happy family,
    Grandma, Grandpa, sons, daughters, Little John,
    wrought-iron benches and swings.

Stifling summer heat.

Peace.

RAVEL'S BOLERO

In the distance, past a blinding dropping sun, I see a hill, trees, a white stone village.
Bold, colorfully dressed maidens come to greet us, you and me, we the soldiers,
    the victors.
Old women and dogs trail behind us, all hurrying down the hill.
We march steadfastly, beating our drums, holding our flag high.
    "The gods were with us!"
Music bangs, people dance, flags whip in a hot breeze.
My heart quickens, the true victory is to come home.
I run, dropping my weapon, forgetting my bandages of dried blood.
"Praise God!" shout the masses.
"Praise God!" we soldiers answer.
They circle around us, kissing, clasping.
"Home! Praise God! Home!"

The ceremony begins, marching, dancing, all of us up the road.

Maidens splashing vases of cold water over us.

Children and dogs prancing in circles at our feet.

Voices rise, "Glorify them! Glorify them!"

Angels sing out through the blackened sky.

Candles light distant windows of those who wait for us.

The priest bears a cross and a patron saint.

We ascend to the candle lights, singing.

Up, up the path. Up, up the steps to the feast.

My breath bursts. I am swept forward, stars swirling above me.

Music, dancing, singing, sweeping me up. Up, up the steps.

Cymbals clash! The exultant moment flashes before me.

There. There it is. I see it. His face.

   "Praise God! I have seen God's face!"

Now it is gone.

Around me . . . friends, family, my wife who is passion's child.

We dance! Embrace! *This* is the victory!

POET

Dear poet,
it is that in you I love,
not only your dancing eyes,
not only your black wavy hair that frames your
      Charles the Second face.
It is the love you give,
your thoughts of roses,
picking up my things,
precious strokes,
tender words.

But then you keep yourself from me
and sleep separately.

I grow dark
and hate your fears of all you want
that keep you from me.

The tears I weep
are they for you or me?
    Us.

Can we love
yet not too much?

Crying does not help
but I still cry.
I feel goodbye.

No words,
nothing said.
I feel you gone.
Whatever we searched for in each other
was not there.

WHITE KNIGHT

Cavalier Mesmer,
your dark bold eyes penetrate to my depth.
When you speak breathe sigh,
I am caught.
It is not strong of me,
but it is love.

My mistake was coming at your whim
    not mine,
letting you be the one to rule.
It was not strong of me,
but it was me with you.

I know you desire my flesh
    I drink yours, too,
but you wish one who lingers like a dream,
a woman separate when apart.

More than the sight of another with you,
it cut me that you lied
and that I am not your pride.
How small I am to you.

I had no chains on you.
It was the other way.
I martyred myself.
Not smart.

Your scent, your way.
Illusion shattered.
Silence sours.
Secrecy binds me.

Our bodies writhing—
the bliss!

One mistake.
    My voice.

I strained at the bit
but kept my place.
I even gave away my dog to please you.

Your life, your way, your time, your place,
your parties, your friends,
        not with me.
Using.

And to think I would have married you.

KING OF CUPS

The Tarot showed me your fair face,
your laughing cobalt eyes,
your chestnut hair crowning a cherub's grin.
I knew you in another life, my love.
we the Lovers unafraid to dream,
embracing tears of sadness and of joy.
Your timeless presence in my House of Wands
stirring my sleeping soul,
waking me the whole night long.
You are my destiny.

WHERE IS THE SUN?

You who need no one
glitter warmly as the sun
and spoil me for everyone.

You sent my moonbeams flying
with your quiet stardust words.
Now this moonchild's crying
because your silence hurts.

You who need no one,
you who are the sun,
what is the shadow from which you run?

NOVEMBER MORNING

Bare brown twigs
scratch scratch scratch
the dewy windowpane above me.
I roll over.

Gingham curtain,
drabwhite sky,
white flakes blowing past.
Cold.

Scratch scratch scratch.
I stuff the heated blanket up under my chin.

MISTER LIGHT EYES

Light in your eyes
soft sweater
soft beard
dancing close.
Mutual minds.

Hopeful again.
Sentimental.
It's been a long time.

I may even let down my walls with you.

VULNERABLE

Trembling to Johnny Mathis,
the passionate tenderness of *Granada, Serenata, La Montana.*
Chilling to the symphonic *Bachianas Brasileiras* Parts I, II, and III.
Feverish with exhilaration.

Green bamboo, candles, incense;
records, books, ten thousand authors.
Rushing wind against my door,
rhythmic ticking grandfather clock.
One brief hour from the world.

Misting my thirsting plants.
My black tortoise-shell cat meowing hello,
brushing up my leg,
curling atop a pillow on the floor.

There are friends,
but wouldn't it be exquisite
	for I am vulnerable today
if the Prince should ride into my life
all manners and brilliance yet gentle more,
and we would frolic on this pleasant afternoon,
vanishing in the sunlight in a naked field of love.

When I least suspect it
and no longer guard my way,
the Prince will ride into my life,
dismount, smile, remove his crown and say,
"It's only me. I thought you'd never notice."
And I will see my heart was blind as me
and there you'll be,
my friend.

I THE FOOL

A phone waits beside me
silent
at a friend's house
alone.

The late show is over.
I toss the wadded Kleenex
onto the hot black logs
and watch the tissue shrivel.

The phone is silent.
I put out the fire
the light
and lock the door.

Slick white streets
slide me home
to a rented rollaway bed
and no phone.

I cry.
Why do I wait for you to call?
I could have anyone.

ANCIENT LOVE

In your face
    bearded reddish brown
    pale blue eyes smiling
    gentle philosopher,
are you as I knew you
somewhere
somewhen
in ancient ages past?

MAN IN SUSPENDERS
AND RED PLAID

Gentle man in thick soft red plaid cotton shirt
thermal underwear and red suspenders,
    broad hairy chest
    tall and strong,
you make me blaze within.
You are a casual man
bold yet shy,
a man at that, no boy or guy,
loving tender.

With wintered hands, you pull me close,
nuzzle me into your lamb's wool coat
and hold me tight
with great
quiet.

I open myself to you,
hoping
     Prince charming on a Christmas sleigh.

DON YOU AGAIN?

We discussed God,
visited your father in the hospital,
you freshly divorced
sensitive to music and poetry.
You praised my writing.
We made love.
I was infatuated.

You never called again.
Ignored me at Summit Singles.
Snubbed.
Used.

Sting.

BEAR HUG

Bear of a man,
a lamb is your soul,
the peace of the inner Christ.
A monk you have been
and I your lady fair.
Often we've been together,
as friends.

The age has arrived to enjoy the *splendors* of life.
Into your large loving arms I arrive
and bless you
for seeing my eyes.

REJECTION RISK

I think perhaps your blue-eyed smile is honest,
your wholesome look of sun more than skin.
I think perhaps your friendly talk is interest—
but I ask anyway
and with a house burgundy and cold draft beer
we begin.

DANGEROUS MAN

I fell into your arms, demon-ridden man,
and you led me down into a deep dark mystery.

Angels delivered me,
saved my sanity and my life.

Yet it was a door
through which you bid me, promising gold and love.

You disappeared
on the run
from men in black who carry guns.
Not my world.

You may be dead,
but a question plagues me:
    Was it real?
    Or merely another longing of my heart?

FEAR

Death is knocking at my door.
Go away.
I don't want to see you.

Death is knocking at my door.
Go away.
Go away.

Dreams,
the poem that prophesied,
the persistent calls these four months from The Silent One.
A dreadful sense of foreboding overshadows me.

Go away.
Play with another life.

Death is knocking at my door.
    Are my books in order?
    Who will publish me?

I'm not ready!
Go away.

Death is knocking at my door.

DREAM HUSBAND

After all these years,
dreaming of the one I left behind?

Dream one, a week ago.
Husband courted me to Cripple Creek
and pleased me with a picnic lunch.
I was amazed.

Dream two, two nights ago.
Fifteen years into the future.
Husband was old and someone else.
Many plain women visited his house,
and I was catty about his habits.

When I opened a closet door, there was a big room.
Husband jumped up from the table, knocking over the chair,
swaying, waving a half-full bottle of whiskey.
"Are you an alcoholic?" I asked.
"Yes," he answered, looking pathetic.
Then he said, "You never gave our marriage a chance."
That wasn't true.

Dream three, last night.
Only the first scene. I could take no more than that.
Showing Husband around my town.
In my present.
I got very impatient with him and lost my temper.

Dream one left me curious.
Dream two left me cautious.

Dream three felt prophetic,
that my love life was in for a great surprise
    soon.

Who would he be? Someone I have known or know?
Someone I have yet to meet?
    No.
    Healing my past.

WAKENED

child in x-rated world
new eyes
no longer in the past

SUNSHINE ON SNOW

The other day when I came home and opened up the door,
there was a card, to my surprise, lying on the floor.
It was from you, a valentine, a few weeks early, too,
and words of love were written there to me from you.

Look to the sky, look to the earth, sunshine on snow.
Look to the sky, look to the earth, all aglow.
Feel the sun warm on your face, warm as my love.
Feel the sun in my embrace and kisses of love.
We have each other on this day, tomorrow too;
but more than that, what can I say to you?
Are we forever, or do we die in time?
Whether we are or whether we're not, at least we've got this time.

Look to the sky, look to the earth, sunshine on snow.
Give me your heart this day, my love, and watch the flowers grow.

I read the card, the letter too, and tried to understand
how you could love me as you do when I feel like a friend.
I am a rose unflowered yet, searching for the rain,
so take my heart and help it grow to take away the pain.
Take my heart and warm it with your sun.
Melt the snow that fills my breath and me you will have won.

SMILE HELLO

It seems I've seen you somewhere,
but I don't remember where.
Was it you I saw this morning
on that cloud up there?
The sky was blue this morning
and the weather fair.
Perhaps you were the angel
smiling down from there.
If so, I understand now
why you smile at me,
and that's why I remember.
Do you remember me?

It seems I've met you somewhere.
Do you remember where?
You look so different, somehow.
Is it your golden hair?
I know I would remember
if you'd smiled at me.
How come we didn't speak then?
Was it silly me?

Is that the way it was then?
We had never met?
How come we didn't talk then
when we could have met?
Perhaps the time has come now.
Say hello to me.

And I will say hello, too.
Do you remember me?

I know I didn't dream you
as I thought I had.
You're standing there beside me
with a drink in hand.
Perhaps it's just this party
and we've never met.
But I know I am willing,
will you hold my hand?

I only wait to say it
because we are new,
and I have tried to say it
but I don't know you.

So, let's pretend to say it.
Oh, hello, do you
remember when we met
at that other party, too?

Oh, yes, the time has come now,
so let's do it right.
We have the magic moment
in our eyes tonight.
So, smile hello this moment
and let's dance tonight.

SILVER STAR

I get horny just thinking about your lean tight body swimming above me,
the caress of your chest hair against my soft white breasts,
your tongue piercing me exquisitely,
in breaths you crying, "Oh, Lady, Lady, Lady."
You sleeping beside me, not snoring, not clinging,
touching thighs or backs throughout our individual dreams.
For once, I am not restless to share my very personal sleep.
Loving, dancing, laughing,
salads, Sloppy Joes, iced teas,
bamboo hanging, burglar locks,
dreams and fantasies.

Then we discovered I like you more than just a little bit.
Something you don't want.

I understand your fear of love.
I have it, too.

I am jealous of the others in your bed.
You ignore me, avoid me.
Then we dance and you introduce me to them like a friend.

I love to watch you dancing,
fluid and sensual in your soft Alaskan shirt.
Days have passed and you've not called
nor dropped down the two flights of stairs.

I long for you lying against me,
pushing pulling thrusting kissing.
I dream of you nightly.

But you are like a silver star,
drawing girls to you like a magnet.
I envy those who have you.
I remember the moments.
You are very desirable.

But you hang loose, my star.
I see we have parted.
      So soon.

If I must be a passing ship,
why is the night so short?

MY SUNDAY AFTERNOON & EVENING AT THE END OF YOUR SKI TRIP

I polished my nails skin hair,
the floors tables sinks.
Arranged pictures posters mirrors calendars,
books and shelves and assorted boxes of junk.
Balanced my checkbook, paid bills, wrote letters long overdue.
Once more polished my nails and prettied myself for you.

Lounging in a flowing silk print gown,
soft and nude beneath,
sipping a hot French coffee,
reading *The Sensuous Woman* at two a.m.

Surprise me with a knock.
I have another cup.

THE OTHER WOMAN
IS A PAIR OF SKIS

Your emptied wine glass
sits on the table where you put it
before you said goodnight
leaving me sleeping.

I dreamed of princes and other lovers wanting me.
You were none of them.
I waited for you
all through the dreams.

This morning I wanted to see your bearded face beside me.
Dreading the empty moment,
I covered my head and stayed in bed,

despite horns honking, clocks ticking, bright sunlight,
and feet stomping overhead.

Tonight I need you with me,
ski-worn body and all.
When you get back from Crested Butte,
come over.

MONARCH

Sitting in the noisy wet ski lodge
    waiting for you
    nursing a cold,
through the window watching you out in the blinding blizzard snowfog,
I leaned on a stool against the wall,
shut my half-doped eyes and dozed.

The table shook,
someone tightening boots.
I opened my eyes
and there you were!

There you were
at the table across the aisle,

stuffing a hot lunch down your face,
 laughing,
 animated,
 patting the wet denim buttocks of the blond beside you.

CONVENTION CITY

Unforgettable week, we four girls who typed ten hours every day . . .
and you, Gemini, all the things we did
    touches of love
    safe feelings far from home.

You renewed hope in myself that
    given time
I will love again.

Eating every food:
Hot corned beef on rye at the Sidewalk Café, roll 43 near Fountain Square, shrimp
    cocktail late at the Playboy Club, room service, a red carnation on my tray.
Chinese pressed duck at Wah Hee, boneless barbecue ribs at the Barn, sausage
    and kraut.

Dimitry's Greek roast leg of lamb, baklava, feda cheese tarts, Greek mud coffee.
Chicken and shrimp flambé at Samuri Japanese Kitchen Steakhouse, hot saki rice
     wine, chopsticks.

The movie *I Never Promised You A Rose Garden*.
The Ice Breaker where I met you, cocktails in the Presidential suite.
Dancing at the Playboy Club, using my bunny key (temporary!).
Horses at Riverdowns! To bet—To win!
The rain—the storms—the lightning—the thunder—the always smogged sky
     missing the clean blue Colorado air and bright clear sunshine.
Kings Island in the sticky hot air:
     Hanna-Barbera Fantasy log ride,
        me covering my eyes with my denim cap and jacket.

Watching the 11-year-olds at Disco Land, envious, I too wanting to dance.
   Girls riding crazy rides, up-down-over-around-forward-backward, looping
   the monorail Screaming Demon.

The Hollywood review.
   Just missing Lion Country Safari, buying out the curio shop, pictures of lions and
   big cats, a little elephant, a sunny Happy Face mug.
Fireworks while we waited at the curb for a bus back to town.

Today, it was over.
We girls finished transcribing the proceedings
packed the office to go
walked to lunch
then walked to shop.
I had missed any messages from you.

I returned to my room, sad, and cried.
Only we girls were left tonight.

Thank you, Gemini, for the note under my door
or I would have missed you entirely to say goodbye.

How lucky she is to have you.
I shall always remember you and Cincinnati.

MR. POLICEMAN

Two extraordinary days
    leaving me longing to be filled again.
Loving strokes starved for,
rekindled metaphysics.

Mr. Bear, they call you on the force
police photographer, arsen squad, explosives expert—
yet aware of mind and soul. What a truly free person you are.

More than beginning lover, beginning friend,
a light to my heart
that seldom any longer loves.
Your eyes crinkle,
your inner warmth reaches through to me.

Our time was brief
yet eternity.
Silly and serious. Your wit frees me.
Your quiet courtesy
allows me space to be.

Cracker's Library, Marguerites, warm white wine, mellow singer-guitarist,
colby cheese and crackers, deep sofas, happy people,
dinners at the Rugby Club and the Tao-Tao.
Adventures in knowing each other.
Cosmic energy drawing us close.
Nights
flesh to flesh
little sleep.
Mornings driving you back to your hotel.

I floated.
I float still.

You went home today.
Once again I stave myself within,
immerse in writing,
the loss flowing with this ink.

Intermittent whims of lunacy.

I HAVE YOUR FACE
TO REMEMBER

There is a light.
It is the sun.
It is the moon.
It is your face I see.

There is a tear.
It is the cloud.
It is the storm
because you're gone from me.

How can I see the light you smile?
How can I see and remember?

I still have tears I've cried for you.
They wet my cheeks and it's December.

The moon has come
and shines into my room.
It's big and round,
a yellow huge balloon.
It is the light
    like you
and makes me smile
    like you,
but you are gone
so in my nights
it is the moon that shines so bright.

The sun shall smile when it is day
tomorrow,
and it is warm and will make me mellow.
The sun is you
        it smiles like you
but since you're gone
all through my days
it is the sun
that helps me wait.

So I go on
        with lights to guide my way.
I have the moon.
I have the sun.
I have your face
to remember.

THE LIONESS DEN

I am the Lioness.

Come into my den of amber light and mellow music.

Sink against the gnu hide draping my sofa bed.

Run your fingers through the thick fake fur below.

Bare your feet.

Savor the delicate wafers and creamy pepper cheese.

Melt a chocolate truffle in your mouth.

Roll the warm wine down your throat.

Blow out the tapered candles
    all but one.

Slip off the sofa.

Relax across the rug.

Tilt your glass again
and lick the edges slowly
     with your tongue.
Stroke my mane of red-gold hair
and listen to me purr.
     Who is the master here?

YOU LIKE MY CAT GYPSY

Tiny dark dance floor, syncopated electronic drummer.
Tequila Collins, scotch and water, half bottle of Beaujolais '71,
    the pink carnation I took home.
Steak ka bob, luncheon special, 30 oz. steaks, people bags to go.

Hot muggy afternoon
side by side
after a late night out before.

You trying to repair my accelerator cable, install a double-chain lock,
    remove the bells from Gypsy's scratching post.
I thanking God the dead cat on the highway wasn't mine.

Two nights and a day.
Over a drink and hors d'oeuvres,
you say you are
    Married.
You felt like love.

BIRTHDAY NO. 30

The little me is creeping out today.
I tried to sleep it through
but headache backache and cat dragged me out.
So here I sit,
trying to become at-one again
and to shake off the numbness.

Shaving my legs for baby silky smooth,
preening my hair for the Lioness who wants to groove.
I will be beautiful tonight
for you,
get back into the me that likes to be alive.

Let's choose a dark and private place before a fireplace.
I know no fire's burning, it's July,
but I'll pretend, for I am lonely,
feeling every year today.

The little me comes out like this sometimes,
but she is not the me that's winning.
For in spite of this depression,
the Better Bigger Me shall stand
on the brink of my existence.
For I have passed the age of childhood,
I am passed the hill,
I am looking to the future as a woman will.

I cannot help but simper
just a little I must do
but I'll be glad to be with you.

Let's celebrate my birthday
    as well I should
and by the time the evening's spent
I'll be the me that's good.
I'll be the me again who's got a life to spend.
I'll be me.
I'll be Me.

THE UMPTEENTH TIME

I've written you a song before,
but it's time to say again
how sad I am that I'm not worth your time.

You say you're sick,
but days ago you said we'd Monday dine,
so where were you at six o'clock, at seven, and at nine?
Not even on the telephone?
I just don't understand.
You couldn't make a call to inform me of your plan?

It really wounded me, you know,
to curl my hair and sit

for someone who would never show.
    I thought I'd have a fit!

Well, no more, sir, I'll wait for you.
You hurt me one last time.
Two years ago when we first met
and last night was a crime.

I still like you.
I'm crazy, too,
but that's no problem, dear.
For I'll not wait another day.
I'll go out when I dare.

And if you call, I'll say hello
and I'll be smiling, too,

for even though I will not wait,
I'll want you when you woo.

So don't get mad because I'm sad,
I simply had to say
how hurt I was to stay at home instead of out to play
    on my birthday.

I would have liked to touch your hand
and dinner would be grand.
But no more tears for me, old man.
I've got the evening planned.

WITHOUT YOU

Driving home
after a day of feasting,
laughter, family, a warm fire,
my breath floats before me inside the frigid car.
Bundled from hat to boot
I feel no chill,
but tears are frozen to my eyes.
You did not call.

Warm white ashes powder the wrought-iron grill
and the dying dust crackles.
Lazy with warm air, I sip Rosé
and sulk into a chair.
Without you.

Tears blind me
in my dark empty bedroom.
Wind howls,
whipping past my window.
Full moon lights into my dark room.
Tears blind me
and I hear my own hollow sigh.
Goodbye.

HOPE

No stars danced for me in your eyes,
no violins played in my heart,
but your o-so-gentle squeeze
set an everlasting spark.

WAKING

Dreamy snow light
crawls across my bed.
Swallowing tears,
I pull cold sheets around me.
You were warm.

A TRUER SELF

MELLOWING BENEATH THE YELLOW HUGE BALLOON

I've forgotten. What does impetuous love feel like?
It tires me anymore.
Frightens me.

The childish Italian, who looked to be a man, was not.
I believed him though—
    until he clamped my heart with chains and nailed me to the floor.

Of all of them—
    the misty-eyed minister Pisces,
    the firey Lancelot Leo,
    the dangerous Dan Scorpio,
    the tall beautiful poet with dancing eyes—

these were the most impressive,
though there were many more,
many in the beginning of divorce.

Slowly I have come around.
I know the score.
But I am no musician.
How do I play the tune of love?

Then I needed quick and passionate, fervent and dashing lovers.
I was a foolish girl seeking the fantasy HIM.
But HE never is.
    Pity.
A hard lesson to learn that princes do not ride here.
    Ever.

No more will I be waiting,
with flowers, perfume, or deep-dish lasagna.
The fall is far too heavy.
It smashes.

Each time I loved
        that fast, that desperately
I hurt a little more
when it was ended.

I shall more than likely fall again,
and harder than before.
I only hope the fall is S L O W.
No more diving off cliffs.
No more.

Love shall find me under the yellow huge balloon,
in a park
alone
reading or writing,
some solitary pleasure I enjoy.

Love shall find me,
but no longer prancing,
that dance is now a bore.

Love shall find me under the yellow huge balloon
by a blue lake
feeding pigeons by the shore.

And when he mellows down beside me
and he quiets but he lingers,

I will be there.
He will do his purpose, as I,
and together we will drift beneath the azure evening sky.

Love shall find me.
I have mellowed.
When he's mellowed, too,
we will both embrace the string that ties
to the yellow huge balloon.

CONCEPTION

Melancholy drags her black silk gown
through the darkened streets of town,
sadly tilting her head down in deep despair.
    What to do? What to do?

Melancholy shirks her black silk gown,
dons a white gown soft as down,
laughs and twirls herself around.
    Much ado! Much ado!

CONVALESCING

Blond oral surgeon,
you dig around inside my cheek
as if I'm a cadaver,
punching holes into my puffy flesh,
draining poison from my mumpy ballooned fever-flushed cheek.
A crazy lunatic gigglelaugh escapes inside my mind.

Mashed potatoes, dressing, giblet gravy, I tongue this Easter dinner.
A sick smell drifts up through my nostrils.
The feverish infection waylays me to my old English rocker.
Limp from an overdose of pain pills, to still my throbbing sutured jaw
      and aching head,

I sit days and days
of sick leave,
contemplating my life.

A change is due!
It's time to end the wasting job!
Back to college,
a new best me!
Growing, learning, leader-to-be.
BA, MA, Ph.D.!

AN ENGAGEMENT OF MY PEERS
IN SEARCH OF MY MISSION

How grateful I am, Manitou Writers, in your cozy cottage room.
How grateful I am for your wisdom of poetdom and publishers, too.
My imagination plays hopscotch on your tattered rug.
To me, this old pink armchair sits at Queen Victoria's hearth.

Slowly and deeply I breathe
    in a yogic way
to still my thundering mind and breath,
a moment's meditation in the john
that I may as an actress read my poems *alive* to you
    the poems that are my children.

There are two parts to me:
My greater consciousness, Jung's universal mind,
  the part of me that knows and exalts my gifts to God;
and the human me that hopes but is unsure
    prays for glory
    feels human woe
    needs words, smiles, understanding of the ins and outs,
    ups and downs of a sensitive soul.
Not for worldwide headlines
    my mission is more than for self
and regardless of anxieties and doubts
is God's unfolding purpose in my life.
    It humbles me.

Therefore, Manitou Writers, with your whiskers and hippy-happy clothes,
two-room yellow cottage and ice-cold aluminum cokes,
thank you.

EVERSHARP

Crouched in a back-splitting leg-cross toe-tingling foot-numbing
    slouch against my beige-brown Indian pillow settee,
I bleer through bloodshot eyes,
pin-prickled scalp and forehead,
knuckles clinched,
rice and warm tea, popcorn and teriyakied beef, coming up.
The words I read are fuzzy,
the TV makes me queasy,
the limitless lint-littered carpet makes me sneezy.

Buried in paint tins and brushes, dulled pencils, crumbled scribbled
    sheets and sheets and sheets; this magazine, that book;
    this agent, that club; this contest, that publisher—
I scream!

My cat romps zoom zoom room to room,
begging consistently for meat.
The plants wilt and droop at my feet.
Through midnights and madness, I complete.
Though my rubber's edge is ended,
I am lead with one more feat.
I am pencil never dulling,
ever sharp and off my feet!

EYES

We are in the beginning time of amazing stories—
but before we each can fly
we must remove our masks.

Human cobwebs
distilleries
plush in our disputes,
fashionable strains of anti-anything,
privy to every pussed indiscretion,
defenseless in our lack of sensibilities,
screaming toneless muses to our mock concerns,
valuing only our lilting steeple glamours,
sovereign in our singularity,
intrepid flinches in a dim present,

strapped mimes in paramour thrones
    sweet spenceless gratings,
congealed animosities turned to might
    incorrigible stingers
        excised
        igniting,
perpetual divestitures of human glum
terrorizing our inner sweetness.

Our carousel song is putrid.
Thieves are mere reflections of our scorn,
limping until even posthumously they hate us.
We are caricatures of our soiled virtueless pliant treasons,
comedic strangers hugging our own vacuous cries and
poultry-stenched bowelless bellies.

Confused meagerlings,
dazzled in our private tinker-toy worlds,
bated and hooked
by our own incipient savagery toward all our fellows,
salted smearing wounds upon each other's cries.

So much for the whimsical little global village,
our once and future dreamdom.

Behind our masks, our eyes.
Look deeply past the imprisoning human hides.
Cross the temporal invisible line.
Embrace a human being before s/he dies.

Other.
That is how we heal our emptiness.

BEFORE I FLY

Before I fly
I am holding myself,
hauling myself along an old familiar track,
spilling the weights of deaths a thousand times,
scourging the aged mockeries of my breast,
cherishing the earth I previously plundered,
relishing all my celebrated lies and treacheries
    breaking the curse that has bound my wings
    and shred my Oracle song.

Before I fly
I am sorting and sizing everything
    one last time,

studying my glories to inscribe them in my soul,
circumscribing all misnomers I have lived by,
shattering denials of my innate good,
consuming all illusions that I thought were good
    but that misled me.
I am sanctioning the little me,
dredging up my countless tomes,
spinning waves of songs still to be born
    in Me.

To fly
I am learning to regret no more what I am not,
    nor please any other than the Greater Me.
To listen
    carefully
and Love.

I am remembering
    Who I Am,
willing to let go of what I know,
accept the eternal changing Tide of life,
gather to a singularity of Mind
    no more threatened by my little me,
embracing the womb of Heaven,
plunging ahead beyond my gloom,
singing my Song
less weary.

The scourge lays broken.
I step above my whys
stride beyond my wrongs
and leap above the horrid monstrosities of my many pasts,
flinging them to the fires of Devotion—
through which I cannot help but Fly!

SATURDAY NIGHTS

Ice cream social, sing-along under the stars. "Hooray!"
White cat staring through closed door.
Laughter, smiles, warm hellos.
Mint chocolate chip, vanilla, Dutch chocolate, homemade cookies.

At dusk, we dissolve from chairs to blankets onto the damp summer grass,
and sing along off the white sheet on the side of the house:
    bouncing-ball tunes of the grand old days—
    strawberry blonds, waltzing Matildas, Nelson Eddy, Kum-bah-ya.
Glory to God.

I left when the games began,
never caring for charades,
back to the Blue House, cream cheese, bagels, and peppermint tea,

bare walls and ceiling bulbs,
square tables, small groups huddled and serene.
Simple people unashamed to speak the name of God.

Humbling
to grow backward
to the years when Spirit enraptured me.

Ray the Good

KINDERLING

Genesee storm rising through my wilted patience.

Cries, temporal insanity, mesmerize my stoned glassy ignored father-self.

Blasphemed child, riddled with raucous memories,

tantalized by once-sought Love,

bestowed a Glory given only once in Love's good name.

Still, no other could have been the pure surrender to infatuation.

No other face, so smiled, could reach the Fear.

Every hope entranced, every deed won, is a passion learned:

    that life is not unloving,

    is not the loss of sane hoped-for kinder lies,

    but is a frank exposition of one's self,

    a hunted ritual revealed.

All dangers of mindset,
reckless seeds of forted creasings,
    buried since Daddy's Girl was stained,
now are less grim, less regarded (intermittently) as a blooded shame.
Tempered shield, plastic sweetness, molded to survive,
now releases Kinderling to undiscovered means of Joy.
Wounded Girl, still partial to corners of despair,
no longer can belie the sacred trust of Greater Ears,
    those unseen saviors who have counseled.
For all the treacherous misleadings of the human sins,
without whom Girl would wander in her pride,
now rises from unfamiliar treads of conscience
a look at persons, people, all seeking the kinder light.

Fatherless Cinderella wrestling all her life,
pockmarked stains on mercy, lies.

Lenses of saintity, reveled hope,
all a guise toward higher glimpses.
But once the guise is worn
        the voices heard
        the saviors known,
Girl stops meandering in prisoned screams.
Girl stops lessening the hoped for Dream.
Girl
        afraid
        afraid
crawls out of dying—and *feels* alight.

Love is like that.
Love warms the inner fright,

heals the wounds
    the deadened flight.
Love is like that.

Love kindles softness.
Weepened strivings stride in strengths unknown.
Love heals the Girl,
    whose heart lay buried in the lies of Father's faces.
Demeanor says it all.
Once love is kindled
    in the inner skies
all else is kindling for a Fire that purifies.
Fresh resolutions
    even now unknown
press outward from the pains,

tread deeply in the wars of him and her.
Blinding courtesies.

All that has been changed
with one kind friend.

Worries
    pummeling
slowly leave the silent stricken Child.
The Girl's mind—soul—refills.
Patience, courage, tresses of inner lights,
    ever so gently beaming their delight,
give the Girl a moment of forgetting all that's lost,

and all that remains
is the knowing that love has been here
        in this wounded heart.

Love has been here.

RELEASING

Mirrors have reflected ancient sores, scabs.
The war-worn soul releases all world worries.
Listens.
Feels the Resonant Self
    the core.

Gestation is of spirit, dharma dreamed,
plays of our own making, pawns or queens.
Whether we limp in havocked residual threshholds
or embrace the Dance
    thrilling
all just stories.

Stature is not what we scheme,
    not in another
    not in a dream or a vision
    nor in any mystery.
The Dance is more than it seems,
    the jest an imaginary dream.
There is no Writer but we who talk it every day,
No stage but we who live it.

God is we who dare to be
our truth
and live it.

FLICKER

In the core of my being
is wisdom.
Where is it now
in this moment?
    Embrace me.

Where is my reason
in this hour?
    Void.
    Vacant.
    Stripped to my soul.

Genuine delight I have known
        unguarded.
Now a vacuous future unfolds.

Life is a thread.
I walk it
        barely.
At times
        Daring.
        Full.

Angels hold me.
Soul I am—
        but human bridles me.
        I fling against social bearings,
        wrestle wedded fear.

Only one answer flickers within me:
    Care.
    More than for the faceless millions,
    heightened dreams.
    One.

Tender child dancing.

CHARACTER

Inner voices of solace, certain,
bid me return now
into definity
of personal sacred character.
Why else love?

My errors were a voice of inner searching,
working outward to my light.
Torching hopes, memories
but reminders of Spirit's value in my life.
My value is not measured by long-forgotten witans,
but more nobly is the revel of sculpturing my own dimension.
Why else love?

Our eagerness betrayed our full affections.
We could not grasp the fairest face we sought.
Your being, whole, pure.
Your character, noble, rare, unblemished.
Such a heart is difficult to leave,
but I must let my visions guide me now.

Grace does not bestow itself on me,
though honor and reason do,
and these shall measure my experience of mortal being
more than any testimony of spiritual sight.

I gave myself to human drama,
for a time forgetting that your destiny and mine
are but notes in a fuller chorus of each soul.

Neither of us blemished, neither whole, both mortal and divine.
We only sought the fullest reach of who we are.

Pain of love's loss, though a maelstrom ridden,
is not a storm untamed.
Love is the essence of our Beauty sparkled to us by another.
Souls passing through the delicacies of honor's region
        to learn our wholeness.
When we travel together with our equal self
        however briefly
we see our inner kingdom.

Love is a song poised on the breath of angels sharing,
a song of remembering that we are what we seek.
How much more noble this than any small refraction of our light.

To seek, to bond, to share
 if but a moment
and to revel in a bliss known only to the gods.

Bittersweet loss of angel's glimpses.
Bittersweet reflection of my inner good.
For though the loss is real in this dear earth,
at least Love once was championed.
And could it have been so fair if I had not been worthy?
For only comes to us not only what we seek but what we are.
Passionate glimpses of my wholest Self.
Tenderness gone from other's arms.

But inner reaches fathom to the stars.
And so I am
And so I am
 reaching.

DEDICATION

Blessings you bestowed on me
    being in my life.
I have lost my fear of loving,
grasped my heart,
ready to embrace the totality of
    Who I Am,
      which I am still discovering.

You gave me a sense of safety,
healed my childhood scars,
opened my heart to the golden beaches
    in my inner skies.

May you be graced with all the joys of Heaven.
May you know only good and truth.
And may you eternally be my friend.

AFTER

Gazing through picture window
framing blue Colorado sky
white clouds drifting by
bare trees of winter budding.
So am I.

Yesterday gloom, madness and despair,
    dark clouds of self-pity.
I prayed, slept, and in this morn
awoke.
In peace.

I know not what transpired in my sleep,
but I am grateful.

Nearer Peace

FLYING

Flying through black void,
seconds through the universe,
tunnel of thoughts and images
whipping through my mind
to the limitless place of
    God.

Where is the world I have seen in darkness but is light?
Reaching up my lean white arms,
reaching up to
    the Universe.

WHOLE

Happy voices chattering laughing
    unified love
    the Voice of God.
Cheerful purpose, blessing-filled peace.
    Divine chill.

STEPMOTHER

Anniversary dinner at Sir Sids,
red napkins tucked in crystal goblets.
Flower child,
red-and-white carnations brought you tears.

Mother, I love you,
 you my dearest part of life through all these years,
 you ever smiling,
 your child-like heart.

You are remembered.
You are loved.

GRANDMOTHER

You raised me, shrunken old woman
with thin white hair in a flat bun with straying hairs,
in a blue-and-white polka-dot polyester dress
that hangs like a flour sack on your sunken frame.
You are nervous, tired, old.

Stepmother left us alone, to visit, returning to Manitou Incline for Father, Uncle,
    and Aunt.
I played George Beverly Shea for you,
remembering your fondness of him during my growing-up years.
As we listened to the songs of the angels watching over us, we talked.
I read you my new poems and illustrated Big Green Dragon book, surprising you.
You only remembered the eleven-year-old you had raised.

I still struggle against the inhibitions, fears, guilts, and anxieties you taught me.
I still fight you and The Family that lingers in my mind:
>   *Get a good job … Be a secretary … Learn to type … Get married.*
I am a writer and an artist. I will be a writer and an artist when I die.
It is difficult overcoming you in my head,
the parent of no encouragement who bestowed no enthusiasm for my life.
You formed me.
I have tried to grow away from that.

In you now, the helplessness of age—forgetting, blind, deaf, arthritic.
Uncle's strong arm walking you,
with your cane, leading you down the steps into the dark Sunbird restaurant.
For you, it was a burden the eleven p.m. dinner at the corner six-seat table
        with a view.

Through the wall-window, above the city lights the near full moon rose.
You watched it glow and rise in seconds over the shadowed hill

—orange, yellow, white—and looked on and off all night. Familiar.

Your daughters and sons ordered for you
    as if you were an infant
    food mild and soft for gumming.
Sometimes during the evening, you shared memories—
    the summer you spent in Europe,
    bright and witty as you must have been
    once.

The dinner was so late, no one ate, but me. I was famished.
You didn't touch your beef brochette, it was too tough,
and the dab of wild rice was not enough,
so you nibbled a slice of watermelon.

Time to end the evening, to say goodbye,
I had not seen you in three years.

To you, the years I lived with you were but ten brief years in your
eighty-decade life.

    They were my childhood.

    They formed me.

You still scoff at my beliefs and my experience of God.

I love God, too. You gave me that at least.

I even share your love of music and of books.

I want to keep the good of you.

I only broke away from the mold you pressed me in.

Already I too say, "I don't have time" and run myself ragged.

But I am learning

    to forgive

    and to see you now

    as You.

MY LANTERN

My closed fingers carry a lantern lit with eternal ethereal oil.
The lantern shall burn brightly all of my days
and always direct me through sunshine or haze.
The lantern will always be in my grasp,
and if I should let go, it will float beside me,
guiding my way.

Wherever I travel down grass-covered tracks, I'll not be alone now,
and more than light shall I find on my path.
For the farther I walk, the more I see
    grass so green, I'll never thirst
    grass so green, I'll never hunger;
    my life shall be fuller than I've yet seen,
    and all I desire will be there for me.

The grass is so green on this track I trod that I'll never want,
for material blessings the lantern brings.

But the greatest sight I see in its light
is neither money, fine foods, nor clothes for a queen.
The grass beneath my feet is sweet and tender.
The grass of my journey has neither fences nor crossroads from here
        to the Doorway.
I've none but plenty the rest of the way,
plenty the pleasures, plenty of my share life's good measures.

Yet with all the joyous leisurely life, I will have more than this.
For in my travels, I have passed the city of thorns.
I have come to a valley of four-leafed wild clover,
        its rich minty fragrance and honey-green a glimpse of Heaven.

Into this valley the lantern leads me,
surrounding me in pure white bliss.
And in this aura of blessing, I receive the peace I seek.
The being of light in the distance
with arms outstretched
waits for me.

SERENITY

My true humanity
    is inner wisdom.
Courageous in some ways,
    blind in others.

Dreams are the window to my soul;
serenity is my chalice
    holding me in a featherlight embrace.
No vision of myself now
other than being what I am:
    giver
    healer
    living the passion of my soul.

More than affection,
more than destiny,
a burst of inner Fire
purifies my imaginary truths.
Serenity enfolds me . . .
and I am grateful.

REFLECTIONS

In one day, on January 11, 1992, between midnight and two a.m. (the 11:11), the following insights into my whole life and whole self came into my mind one at a time. This inspirational vision from my higher mind revealed my human struggle from quenching my shadows to embracing my wholeness as a spiritual being.

ABYSS

Consciousness is a teacher.
As we realize it, we stumble through mazes of self-quiet,
fend off sleepy sadnesses and grievous pomposities,
journeying in Society as a sainted martyr.

Why seek Heaven when all is here?
Why yearn Peace when letting it breathe is so near?
I cannot say.
I too wander in my own abyss,
cry in my reasonings.

How can I find peace when I shun it so vigorously each hour?
Perhaps I only fail to offer it my succor.

Perhaps I only meet it in my deepest angers.
Unable to touch the pit.
Lord.

Christ is bleeding.
In my heart
I *know* life.
Is it not simplicity,
consciousness,
freedom to expand?

All that beckons is the fragrance of Purpose
        diving into Heaven's easefulness.
All that carves me is my own uncertain pleasantries of justice.

Oh, yes,
Heaven is my great desire.
Heaven is the seeking of
youth.
   Gone.
   Forever.

So, that's it.
Perhaps now I can stop the madness
and walk in a real life
   here on earth.

SHADOWS

Fear is my brother
jaundicing my bosom.
Quiet eludes my deepest
whole.
Perhaps I am only now
seeing
my Self.

Can I saunter aimless in the World's jaws?
Is it not careless to ignore Wrath?

Forget only pain, I say
in my hidden prism.
Forget not calm surrender,

nor flight in
    in
I can't quite remember.

All right, I wander now in my deep.
But I have *known* life
    fully.
I am only now really seeing
Consciousness.
Who I am.
    in the Womb.
    yet to find the way
    so far
    so far
    so far.
    Candle light dreams.

Forgive me,
Soul.
Forgive me.
I have tried.

Curtains hang on
to my heart
my flesh
my unbeacon.
I live to see You. BE You.
See me. See Me.

Quiet curses my true Nature which ails now.
Quiet is only a cheap escape from joy in Soul
through love.

So I find.
So I find
parades of shadows in my mind
reeking of jestures.
And so I see
my own real Nature still hides from me.

SCRUTINY

I scrutinize myself
    frigid
    barren
    sole,
born into unripened soil, gleaned earth,
restitute of personal honor.

Fortune has yet to sallie in my sun.
    Though Good has. Joy has.
        Peeking.

Learned wisdoms soothsayer
all quite plausible origins of Thought.

But just how important is it
if life is failed?

Burdens relish this foundling's lithe grasp of hope.
Surely there is more to being human?

Caring is an empty womb.
Unspoiled is that chaste perfect blossom
     quite unlike my tortuous death dreams.

Can any of us conquer madness?
It willingly flaunts itself
in every gaping horror of our lives
     day
     to
     day

to

day.

How do we plunge our barest fringes of certainty
into such vile leaches of the Just standards of this world?
Religion mocks the Christs it stands for.
Churches beam only to those who mourn sanctity.
Lifestyles of the Rich deprive us of our faintest grasp of dignity.
We aspire
    not to Soul
but soulless cringe
in caverns of inhuman cravings
    pitted
    dense
    frays
    of yesteryears.

Cool
tough
prisms shattered.
In it, somewhere
meaning,
focus.

Reason creases
barely.
Only listening
is She Who Walks in Light.
Soul.
Soul listens.
Soul cares.
Only.

PLEDGES

Visions catch the unaware,
leaping
caressing
relishing unresolved dharma,
cleansing the whole.
Reaching.

Smiles wane.
Smiles soften.
Smiles heal.
Inner touches.

Forgiveness heals the center.
Aloneness heals the center.
Reality leaps into a new divinity of hope.

Shuddering is that shadow
lingering but frail,
for glaring to it is a tide of birth
sweeping from the unborn
to a vista of possibility.

Pledges to hold high all that honors.
Pledges buried in persuasive self-defeats.
Yet wounded not am I,
for even then
now
a last look back at pain.
No longer taunted by past errors,
no longer teased by future's treats.
Ready to stand and BE
Just what I am.

DEEPEN

Pledged to serenity
on the wings of Heaven's song,
I bow now
to my inner Me
and thank all Mysteries
that I can be
so human
    with frail stirless risings
yet still understood by the knowing inner self
of all to be.

All that I could be
already can I be.

All that I would be
already see.
All that I dare to become
I am now.
I can be.
I am.

Hell is charred sweetness
lost innocence
caressed temptations.

It is time to be.
Just be.
That is all.

Curtains lift from the flesh
and hearts deepen
and all the shadows crawl away,
for even in the shallow cells of self-bequeathed curses is
    release.

Consciousness tenderly dances
around the aspects of the world-weary wanderer in
frozen flight.
    Sculptured
    melting
    ice.

Tethers fray.
The harness of Social wearings
splits
and breaks.

Cast-iron
soldered
freakish Truths
shatter
crisisless in the crystalline reflection of the higher truth.
    Just be.

No judgment day disposes.
No fire putrefies the scars of ageless pasts.
    Just be.

Meekly allow the pain to fall away.
Through
beyond
comes self-acceptance
and self-love.

Just BE.

DARE

Quickened desperation clings,
rasping at its last grasping breath.
So be it.
Over.
Death to the bedeviled little overwhelmed youthless child.

Crested salutations,
eagle high,
leap timeless
and bequeath Fire
in the corded heart.
The Fire spins flames of feathers and winds
through vaulted spires
toward rising kindled seed.

The Fire rushes birth,
sea to fullest light.
Pressed
pressed
surging
into weathered courage.

Bathed in Presences of tender Sight
wells out my songbird poise,
    and weary less
I climb the restless skies of tender years
    to break clean and chart anew
    the unforeseen.

Poised
eagle dared
Flight.

Pressed
pressed
surging forth,
bathing in
    at last
deepest gratitude for life.

Poised
eagle high
surging forth.
Fired.

Winging ascending, climbing hills and skies
    for all that is there.
Ever curious.

Spiraling levels aware
    beyond the dearth of platitudes
    into the *alive* sensation of
    BEING.

FRUIT

Phantasies blissfully meander in uncertain dreams,
only tear screeching inner halls.
Crusted sallow bearings
cheek despair
fondle longing's bellies.
Personality clings to frigid windows of false airs.
Persuasive sorrows needle ancient sores
and prick spurned daunted youth.

Even so, settling is, once and for all, forgiveness.
For all the tauntings of mistaken journeys
and lives-long miseries bought,
only a pause away is sweet height,
sweet surrender.

Holy sense.

And in all the aged prisons of misguided reasons,
in all the tortured self-misplighted truths,
in all the denied denounced passionate glimpses of
    fuckled youth
is a pause
a glow
bearing itself outward from within.
A shell
    breaking
    bursting,
quickened laughing resonant joy.
Fruition of the falsely unprepared.

Golden dawn
spreading Fire through old despair
and purging all old fear.

Fruition
at last
here.

BIRTH

Kindled spirit,
flame tendered from bemuddled bewildered youth,
etched forever in ages remembered.
Splendid favor,
crescent miracle of holy tinctured truth,
birthed
at last.

Realms seasons dauntless nights of scented wanderings in flight,
cautioned plagiarings in captivity,
listless lethargic little me
    so carefully toyed
eased
at last.

Castrated hope
spurned desire
wellspring sighed,
healed
at last.

Seasons of life,
quickening minds and souls
　　　wisdom teacher,
all spells of higher comprehension
cast in a better light
　　　for all life's learning.
　　　Noblesse oblige.

Sultry sensual self arise,
love is bending softly

and all sense of self renews
in the unbridled essence of devotion.

Listen well, little sister.
Youth is but a moment.
Wisdom is timeless truth
        taught not elsewhere but in experience.
All that winds itself like threads through the human heart
        seeming to tug and strangle
        are merely unfamiliar strands of a fuller tapestry
        of devoted being.
When one has released all false definitions of how to joy
and gratefully surrenders the heart
in devotion to sensibilities of silent good,
then that one releases the little self

and breathes
    fresh
    kind
    dear Life
into the bosom of quickened awakening self-look.
That one forgets the little self
    and beyond
sees the vastness of creation,
to lift beyond the mire of woebegotten fames
into the spectacular vistas of creative sight
and the fathomless reaches of perfect Flight.

As eagles rise,
so does the soul who dares to live
    beyond
in unbridled caring.

Take care
and know the true meaning of one who
lives.

GREETING

Prisms of crystalline clarity rise in me now.
Pleasure is Gentleness weaving her essence through me.
Serendipity is in every moment.
If only I but know it, it is there,
    wrestling to free me
    bequeath to me
    all that I dare
    to believe in me.

Poise in me
care in me.
Love.
For the Beauty *is* there
if I but only see it.

How quaint I am in my antiquated sidelong glances
    at *being.*
How flavorful are my timid despairs.

Time to pack it up and send it off
greeting
a new day!

THE
SACRED NOW

THE SACRED NOW

Restoration
of the inner knowing
comes in the stillness.
    Remembrance
    of that peace
    that is The Only Life.

In this,
renewed,
I come back to
mySelf
    again.

Blessed.
Healing.
Once more recreating my life.
What will it be?

What will *I* be?
Why can't I just *be*?

Coming back upon
the Sacred Path,
angels' voices
guide my way:

Hope.
Believe.
Faith.
Trust.
Heart.

I want to believe. I want to.

Believe.
Sometimes you just have to believe.

ISBN 1412072530

9 781412 072533